THE TRAVEL DIARIES (OF A KID WHO HATES TRAVELLING)

DAIVIK DAS

Made with ♥ on the Notion Press Platform
www.notionpress.com

I want to dedicate this book to my parents and grandparents who always try to make the best out of me.. I want to dedicate also to my English teacher, Nidhi ma'am who made my English skills much better.

Contents

Preface

Me, an 8th grade boy who people thought had some writing skills made me publish this book. My writing journey started around the age of 8-9yrs, during the peak of the Covid wave. My grandfather used to give me topics on what I should write about. I had found a nice diary in which I used to write the points about the topics which my grandfather used to say (I still have the diary). In grade 5, I had applied for a story-writing contest. I had won the first place. Since then, I started writing real stories. I have a book in which I write all my fictional stories. My uncle had given me a travel diary in which I write all my travels. I started completing notebooks with stories. Then one day I had bought a book. When I saw the author, I saw it was a boy almost my age who had published a book. Till that time, I didn't know that kids could publish books. Once I saw it, I knew I had to publish. Me, and my parents thought is better to go one step at a time and try to publish my travel diaries. And let me say this first, I HATE travelling. I feel dizzy and feel to vomit. You will know more about that when you read the book. So I thought to add some jokes to my boring old travelogues written in my diary, and make it fun to read. I hope you will like this book!

Acknowledgements

My father helped me a lot in publishing this book. My grandfather also made some adjustments to my book. If it weren't for them, my book would be trash. My mother also reminded few parts of my journey which I had totally forgotten. Thanks to them, this book is a success.

ONE

THE FIRST TRIP

We went to Kerala and the district is Wayanad. This is the first time we went alone in a trip. (Or usually we'd go with our friends or relatives). I always hate road trips for very long distances because I vomit. Bengaluru to Wayanad is very long. But I had no choice but to go. So we went on one unlucky day at 8:30AM. We saw many trees as usual. Then we stopped for eating lunch. After that we again started the onward journey. It took a long time, but I finally reached. In Wayanad our car did some time off-roading. My father had booked a home stay at Wayanad. We rested the whole day as my father was driving for long. The next day we visited many places like, Banasura dam, spice garden, tea plants and tea museum.

Our first stop was in Banasura dam. There I rode bumper cars because it is fun. Then we went to the dam there I saw a zip line. My father was telling me to sit on it but I was scared so I didn't ride it. In the dam, there were a lot of stairs to climb and a lot to walk. But the scenery around the dam was very beautiful. After that we went to spice garden.

Spice garden was a bit lot boring than I had expected. I saw many types of plants. Some I knew, some I didn't, and some were confusing. I now only remember two plants: Pepper, and Hibiscus.

I was really hungry, so we went to a restaurant and had food. Then we went to the tea garden. There were gardens full of tea plants but for me it was boring. After this we went to the Tea Museum. There were many old things like: tea strainer, tea grinder, varieties tea powder etc. I drank some chocolate milk and then we headed back to the home stay. There I played in the swimming pool! After returning back from pool I took a good bath.

Today was a sad day because I was leaving the home stay and going back to Bangalore. I was ready before my parents. After my parents were ready we gave the keys to the owner and headed to Bangalore. We had taken a break in between the journey. Actually, the owner of the homestay had recommended us to visit the Edakkal cave because it will be on the way to Bangalore. But we were hungry were not so interested for a cave. And if you askme to choose a cave or a restaurant after a long trip, I'd choose restaurant and that's exactly what we did. That restaurant was 80 years old wooden building. My mother had bought some Kerala spices on the way and. Then again after a long time on road we reached home, Bangalore.

● 3 ●

TWO

THE DIFFICULT TRIP (WITH A FRIEND)

As you know I hate long road trips but I had a friend with me so I was somewhat interested to go. My friend's name is Srijith. Luckily this time I did not vomit as my friend was with me. We had a break on the way. I and Srijith had bought juice. As usual after a long time we finally reached. The journey was 6 hours and the place is Chikmagalur. This time we stayed in a resort. Srijith and his family stayed in the room next to our's.

The next day was Saturday. We had planned to go to Coffee Museum but it had been closed. Though we had planned to go to Mullayanagiri hill at first, we cancelled it later. But as the Coffee Museum was closed, we went ahead with the Mullayanagiri hill trip (we obviously can't sit inside the room and sleep right?). So we went to the base of the hill by our car and then hired a jeep to go to the top of the hill. The speed of the jeep was fast (or that's what it seemed so). It was so fast that I thought while it was going through the winding path of the hill, the jeep would tip and fall down. But it didn't. After keeping my soul and body together, we finally reached. But wait! Not yet. We still had to climb like 500 steps. After climbing like probably 50-100 steps we felt tired. Me and Srijith wanted to climb more but our parents didn't allow us.

Oh wait! I almost forgot to say that we went to the swimming pool twice since the day we arrived here.

Climbing down the hill by the jeep was not at all scary. It was almost 2:30PM and we would reach resort at 3:00PM, so we thought to refill our stomachs by going to restaurant. That night, me and Srijith were playing with the toys we bought with us.

The next day was a bit sad because we were leaving today. Me and Srijith had made some new friends in the resort. We had seen some indoor games and gym. Cycling was also there. So we also did some cycling. Then we went to our home in Bangalore. Again after a long drive time, we reached home. Srijith went in his car to his home. Wait! I almost forgot to say something else! Me and Srijith had also visited the Mahatma Gandhi park and also did a train ride at Chikmangalur.

THREE

DEVOTIONAL TRIP (BORING)

It was a very sunny morning in the month of April. Puttaparthi is located in Andhra Pradesh which is very, very far from Bangalore and we were going there. Actually we are going to Prashanthi Nilayam to do puja to Satya Sai Baba. So we started at 5:30AM (I think). Now as I said Andhra Pradesh is far (approximately 3hr 45min). I was feeling nervous because my vomit may come during the travel. But luckily we had a few stops in the middle which somehow stopped my nausea feeling. We then reached Puttaparthi. The place is small. We entered the main entrance gate of the ashram, showed some papers and looked for the accommodation office. After driving a while we found it. They gave us the keys for our room. Near the accommodation office we saw a canteen and my mother bought some snacks from there. We finally found the building in which we were going to stay. We went to our room. After washing up a bit we ate the snacks and later went to the canteen to eat lunch. My mother went to the North canteen and father and I went to the South canteen.

After eating lunch, we came back to our room and went to sleep.

Then in the evening we woke up and went to "Sai Kulwant hall" during veda chanting. We did some boring dhyana. (dhyana means you just sit quietly and think about God) (This was kind of boring). After the Darshan of Satya Sai Baba samadhi, we had no work, so we went to our room, drank some water, and relaxed. Later we went for dinner.

This time, I went to the North canteen. It wasn't as good as the south canteen. Then we went back to our room and went to sleep. The next day morning, after my mother and father finished watching mobile, we went to have our breakfast. After licking the food off, we went for the morning darshan. After that we again had no work so we went back to eat lunch. This time I ate from the south canteen because I could eat the fastest there. We quickly ate lunch and bought a lot of cake and then we went to our room. There we slept a little and then we started our return journey. We had to stop at a place between the border of Andhra Pradesh and Karnataka (Puttaparthi is in Andhra Pradesh) to drink some coconut water. Again we had to stop

to refuel ourselves with tea and snacks. Finally after all that,
we reached home.

FOUR

OLD HASSAN TRIP

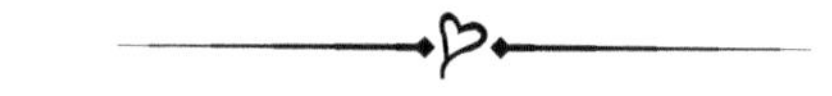

So as usual we have another trip which I think was very, very long. I didn't know where we are going.

After some time, we reached a hotel. It was a bit small and cramped but it looked good (from the outside). I realized we were in Hassan. After getting the key to our room my mother and father went in the lift while I went through the stairs. But what was this! Instead of the first floor there was this "Zest" written there and when I went to the next floor there was some storage. Then finally the next floor was the first floor. So by hook or crook I reached my room. The room though was nice but really cramped. Then after sometime we had ordered lunch from room. After somehow eating lunch at that place we went for a nap.

After the nap I realized we were going somewhere I didn't know. So we had to go through some zig-zag road. We came to a river bed kind of place. There was a ruined church which looked scary at night. It was in Gothic style. There was a river and a bridge near to it. Actually, the ruins of the church were on the river bank. A lot of people weren't there. I had taken my camera as well to take pictures.

The next place where we were going was a lake but due to some drizzling we abandoned the plan. Then we finally went back to the hotel room and dozed off. The next day I woke up feeling very soggy. I was feeling homesick. I brushed my teeth and got ready. Then we ate some breakfast.

After some honourable hours of sleep in the car we finally reached the Chenna Keshava temple of God Vishnu. The temple was okay. But a lot of people asked us to take their photos in the temple. The idols in the temple were massive. How did they fit it in? Then we went to this Hoysaleswara temple of Shiva. Both of these temples are more than 1000 years old. Both these temples were magnificient. But there was not much to see. I only saw some swimming turtles on the water inside the temple premises. Then after sometime we came back to our hotel. We ate lunch and came back home. The trip was not so great this time. Oops! I almost forgot to say that we had to climb 500 steps on a mountain to a Jain monument which was definitely boring. There were another 2000 steps to reach the temple but my parents didn't have the energy to climb.

FIVE

A Trip of Waking Up Early (Everytime)

Again it is another trip to a place which I don't know. (I don't know where we are going at first but then at the last moment they will tell me). For some strange reason I feel like a luggage. They take me wherever they want. Probably like a living, eating and sleeping luggage. Now back to the trip. I had to wake up at 3:00AM for the flight! Normally I wouldn't mind this but this time it was different. I didn't take bath in the morning as our flight was at 9:00AM (don't ask me why they woke me up literally 6hrs before our flight). One thing that was different is that in this trip my grandparents accompanied us.

We quickly reached the airport went in the plane and reached Trivandrum. I don't know how the plane's tire didn't catch fire as it was really hot outside. Soon we reached Trivandrum, in Bangalore there was a lot of wind rain and cool weather that we couldn't experience at Trivandrum. Now we reached the hotel in a big taxi. We reached the hotel very quickly. As soon as we entered, we felt very cold (which is completely normal because of the ACs present inside the hotel lobby and the hot weather outside). Now we had 2 rooms- one for my grandparents and one for my parents. So we came to stay here for two days. But wait, everything can't be perfect so we had a problem. They took a lot of time to give the room keys. I don't know why but I feel like when we asked the hotel people about our room I think they started constructing it using bricks and cement. Finally after hours of wait we got one room. But we knew it's going to take another eternity to give us the second room, so we went to have lunch. After the lunch we went to our rooms and slept for some time. I slept with my grandparents. After waking up we went to a beach which was dirty. I put so much dirt in my crocs that whenever I wore them it felt like ants were biting me in the water. We came back to the hotel and I washed my crocs. Then I walked for some time so that it would dry off. We went to have dinner at the restaurant in the Hotel. The restaurant staffs were kind and let us taste the food to check if it was spicy before ordering the same.

The next day I had to wake up at 3:00 AM again but why? Because we had to go to a very famous temple, Shree Padmanabhaswamy Temple. Okay till now it was understandable. But wait! I had to wear dhoti that early in the morning and all that before sunrise. Well I had to go because as my entire family were awake except the sun. So after reaching the temple we had to find a way to see the diety and then to search for the exit. But wait after the temple, there is a big discussion in our room. Let us see what is going on here.

Papa: I hope everything is ok

Mama: That Vishnu statue is so big I couldn't see it properly

Papa: Do you want to go again?

Mama: no, as there is a long line. It is going to take a lot of time

Papa: I have heard about a special darshan in which you can give more money and cross the line

Mama: but we will see the same thing again

Papa: Yes, but hgbjugdskjugvsduyfdndgfvytuftcmnfcugtmtu

Mama: unyfurcnunygyjfytrwertghvcdftyujk

Grandmother: nfuybnye7bng65eugbftvbido

So as you can see this important discussion went for hours-while sitting, while eating, while sleeping.

Meanwhile I kind of got angry on my grandfather because he is always asking me irritating question like-why are you eating fast, Why are you eating slow, why should you sleep, why should you have wooden doors, why infinity is called infinity and other random questions. So as we had

woken up very early we went to sleep after breakfast. Then we had lunch and again went to sleep. (I know you're thinking that we are the laziest people on the face of earth). After we woke up we went to a place where there was a lighthouse. It did take some a lot of time to reach. And after that we reached the lighthouse which was made for one person but as we are greedy humans we all will still go up to the lighthouse. So that means that there was crowd along with narrow stairs as we went up. I mean there were so many people, they had to install a small lift there to go to the top. Then we had to climb a very narrow wooden ladder to go up. After somehow climbing it up we took some photos and came down. My grandfather stayed back near the car and my grandmother couldn't climb the narrow stairs so she stayed in the bottom of the lighthouse. Now we went to another beach which was much cleaner than the first one. And this time my shoes didn't get much dirty as the last time. But sadly my father's shoes got wet.

After all that we had dinner. Again the important discussion was going on. Luckily at the last moment, after using the brain cells left in their brain they decided that we won't go because we would see the same thing. The next day I again had to wake up early. *Why?* Because this time I was returning to home. I was excited to go back home as I've been waking up at 3:00AM (which is completely normal according to a kid like me)

We packed up and had breakfast. The taxi came fast. Then he put our luggage on the roof of the car without any belt to secure it. So as soon as I reached the airport, I checked if the bags had flown away or not. After going to the boarding gate the airport looked small and different. Later we reached the plane. They had put gallons of humidifiers that we couldn't see ourselves due to the vapours. After hunting for our seat we finally sat down and then finally reached Bangalore.

SIX

A Trip Far From Home

This trip we had decided to go to Shirdi (a city in Maharashtra state). We had gone to Shirdi by flight. The airport was very huge. After that we had a taxi waiting for us. I realized we weren't in Shirdi. We were in Pune. It was normal for me to land somewhere without anyone telling me (because my parents will take me wherever they want). So now as we were in Pune, we were obviously staying at a hotel for a day or two before going to Shirdi. As expected this is what happened. We went to Shirdi from Pune in a car. We were going to an ashram to stay.

After reaching the place, my brain cells were cooked because I couldn't feel my fingers or toes working properly. And in that situation, my father left us to sit on a bench while he did the registration and stuff.

I didn't know that the 'registration and stuff' would take so much of time that my legs were starting to pain. (I was sitting on a bench). Finally after an hour I think we headed to our rooms I was thinking as soon as I reach the rooms I would doze off. But I was wrong (as always). The block was 1km away from the registration office. This means we had to walk for a 1000m to reach. When we reached our block, we had to get our keys from the front guy sitting there. We showed the bill, got the keys and rocketed to our room. We reached there and took a bath.

After bathing we went to have darshan. But as the bus was free, it was stuffed with people. So we decided to go on an auto rickshaw.

After the darshan, it was evening. So we decided to have dinner. As we had wasted our money in the rickshaw ride, we thought to have the free dinner which was given in the ashram (staying place).

The next day we went to the Grishneshwar Jyotiling. (Don't try to spell it you'll fail). But we had to stand in a queue for 4 hours. My legs had started to feel like jelly. But in the temple, half of the country's population was there, so that meant I could lean on other people and they wouldn't realise who was pushing.

During the bad hours of standing in the crowd, it started raining. Luckily we had an umbrella as my mother bought one. So we were saved from getting wet. Then we came out of the temple and ate in a small restaurant. After eating, we went to the Ellora cave which is one of the most popular places in India. It was huge. Then we came back to the ashram. But as we didn't eat properly for the day, we thought to eat in a restaurant again. After eating we came back to our room and slept.

The next day we woke up early. Why? This time we were going home. So we quickly got ready for our last darshan. It started raining heavily. We called an autorickshaw and it dropped us at the temple.

After we came back from the temple, we ate breakfast in a restaurant. But the problem was that my father didn't have any cash with him after eating and the restaurant only accepts cash. So my father had to go out in the rain with the umbrella to find bank ATM for withdrawing cash. Luckily after a while, my father came back. After eating breakfast we went to sleep. We woke up early so we went to sleep. If you think we are just lazy, I will come to your house and make you do your homework). But as our nightmare, our flight got cancelled. So we had to book another flight to go home.

It was still raining. We packed up, called the taxi, and deposited the keys.

It started raining again, but this time we were in the taxi. So that means:

Me: 1

Rain: 0

When we reached the airport, it again stopped raining surprisingly. When we finished the check-in, there was this group of people who asked us to smile for a picture for Indigo's happy journeys something. We took the picture and went our way. It started raining again. The airport was small. There were only two gates-1&2. Our flight departure was from gate one. But there was a problem. Our seats were at three different places in the flight. Luckily, there was this lady who helped us get our seats to next to each other. It was still raining. So when we had to reach the plane, there were people covering our heads with umbrellas so we won't get wet. After we reached the plane, the plane started taking off in heavy rain. I was taking pictures from the window. The plane went above the clouds and it stopped raining. After sometime, we reached Bangalore

SEVEN

THE HILLY RIDE

So today we had another trip, (Like I had said these people take me wherever they want) which I didn't want to go because it was a road trip. As you already read the title, we were going to Mangalore…from Bangalore, nice rhyming. Anyways as I was saying, we had a mid stop at Mysore while we were going to Mangalore. My mother told me that she and my father had a surprise. I had totally forgotten about it because I know their surprises would be a restaurant or they had just got a gift for me (which would be most likely books). But this was different. When we reached that place, I thought we reached the hotel. Because, obviously we were going to stay at a hotel for a night at Mysore before going to Bangalore. But this "hotel" looked different. It looked like a car tyre. Then my mother said that it wasn't the hotel but a car museum. I love cars. But I hate history. So when you mix history and cars, I don't know what happens. But luckily, it was not bad and this was my surprise.

I saw TONS of cars. Big cars, small cars, massive cars, you name it. They had kept a few bikes too. I saw cars that were bigger than cars today. No, not monster trucks but normal passenger vehicles. I saw some modern cars too, I knew almost all of their names. After that we saw a door. We entered it and saw all the old artifacts and "Tullu kitchenware". It was all about old things and all (history), which I was not interested obviously. Then we reached Mysore. We stayed at a hotel there. Now, the thing is that whenever we go to a hotel or resort we have some important things to do there, that is-

-As soon as we reach, ask for extra towels

-Steal all the tea and coffee powders (which were meant to be used by us)

-Steal the shampoo and soap

- Switch on the TV to check if it works

These are only 5 things which I listed out here, but actually we do more things. Sadly it is not the right time to talk these things here.

Then we ordered food in their restaurant. After eating we were back to the room. I and my mother wanted to explore the hotel. We saw a swimming pool, café, gaming place and all. But we didn't have time for all that so we went back to our room.

The next morning, everything went smoothly. We ate breakfast, got our luggage and checked-out of the hotel. But there was a problem. As we were leaving for Mangalore, we realized the trip will be hilly. So we had to go through twists 'n' turns a lot. I had vomited twice while going.

My mother also started to feel uneasy; it was time to take a break. My father was forcing me to eat toffees. I would have vomited if I would have eaten anything else. Tick-tock and it was already noon. My father parked his car in the side and we all had fruit 'n' nut cake. Only 1-2 hours was left for us to reach Mangalore. When I was small, I used to ask my father how much time would the journey take which we were going and if he said it's more than two hours, I would feel vomiting there. This trip was 5 hours. Luckily I'm not a small kid anymore because if I would have then I would have become jelly after reaching the place. Anyways as I was saying we had finally reached the place. It was a home stay called "The Little Prince". The home stay owner was Christian and Christmas was coming soon. So everywhere was Christmas spirit (I don't mean people wearing Santa hats and all). But a PROPER Christmas like Lord Jesus prayers and lightings. We were discussing about dinner and decided to have it in a restaurant. We asked the owner's brother, Jason. He is probably the backbone of the Little Prince home stay. He wakes up at 5AM to check the water and all. We asked him for a restaurant nearby. He said there's a restaurant on the seashore. We went there, it was a posh restaurant. We first thought it was a resort. But it wasn't and inside was freezing for me. We were sitting directly under the AC. I was wondering when the food would arrive as recently, I had learnt in science that if we eat food it makes energy and HEAT. And for the moment, HEAT was much needed. I wasn't much hungry. The hunger had died in the cold. While we were waiting, there was a guy who was singing. My mom didn't like how he was singing so we stopped the discussion on it. Finally, the food came and it tasted good. But the thing is that, next the bill came which was not good because it was too expensive. Anyways we then went back to our homestay and slept.zzzz

Today we had some serious travelling. We had asked Jason for a driver for the day. The driver came, when we were having breakfast. After finishing our breakfast we went to Murudeshwar Shiva temple. It was on a hill slope. We went in the queue. After we reached the temple we were pushed out by other people because "half of the world's population was there". Then we were starving. So I was like lets eat in a restaurant. My mother and father both were angry because they were hungry. We then found a restaurant which was more congested than the Vande bharat. We had to wait for an eternity before we could finally sit down to eat. After the lunch we went to Udipi temple of lord Krishna. It looked like a campus. We went in only to find that they were worshipping some random guru. We knew we were in the wrong place so we waited until another worshipper came and we followed him. There we had a queue one for free with the- wait for 10 hrs for your turn or the second on pay Rs 200 per person and reach in minutes to deity. So we opted for the second one. There was again a short queue. It didn't take much time to reach the deity. As it was night, there were a lot of diyas. And as there were a lot of diyas, the temperature was hot and so we were sweating a lot. We tried to see the idol through the holes in the walls. So one couldn't really see properly. After the darshan, we went out of the temple and we roamed around a bit. We saw another temple (you can't really call it a temple). It was the house of the guy who directed the construction of the temple. As the temple was really very old, that guy's house looked kind of temple. We went inside and there this eerie silence. All the other people had left except, me, my father and mother. The room was dark. I started getting goose bump and before you know I was scared. I saw my father, I think he was scared just as me but he didn't show it on his face. We quickly came out. I will next time remember that not to enter a dead person house.

After all that we came back to our homestay, it had become night. So we were desperate to go to bed. We reached the room, we were relieved, but I felt bad for the driver as he still had to go back to his home. Anyway, we orderd our dinner from homestay's cafeteria. But what was this! there was no salt in any food. I mean literally not a single grain of salt in the food. And when I tasted it, it was horrible. I mean when you eat a food item and you know what is going to taste like but when you eat it, the taste just doesn't get registered by our brain if it tasted different. So while I was eating, my father had to get extra salt so that I can continue eating and won't barf up. But my father brought back crystal salt, which I had never eaten in my life. But once I tasted the salt, it was better that normal salt. While I was eating, I saw some random people entering the home stay dressed in Santa clause clothes.. They danced around the home stay and luckily they didn't see me or come when I was eating or else, I would have been embarrassed. I saw them leaving and finished my dinner and went to sleep.

The next day, we didn't have any plan, so we went to the beach which I kind of regretted. I got wet in the sea (my mother made me wet). And while I was climbing a rock in the shore, I should have known that there were slippery algae on the rock on which I slipped and fell and hurt my leg. Then after we came back to eat lunch at the homestay and went to take short nap. When I woke up, it was dark outside. I thought to roam around a bit. I saw these kids and thought to play with them. After that we ate dinner. After dinner, they started a bon fire, with coconut shells! I wasn't sure if it would light up. But as it is a natural material, I thought it would light up. And it did. When it did we knew it from our room already, because of the music they had put. After sometime, people went back to their rooms because they were tired (I think). But I played with the small guy for sometime. My mother told I needed to get some sleep because we were leaving the next day. So I had to go and sleep for the night.

The next day it was home time. I had to wake up early, which I didn't mind this time because I had got a goodnight's sleep. I and my father saw some peacocks and eagles.

Mangalore is almost like Kerala. All these jungles everywhere and putting coconuts in almost every food. Even the language is a mixture of Malayalam and something which is called "Tulu". That's why we saw the peacocks because of the jungles. We ate some Mangalore buns which were good. My father said we had to leave early today because this time, we were going straight to Bangalore, no stops in the middle.

That sickened me. I had felt terrible when we were going to Mangalore to Mysore. And now we will go non-stop (or that's what I thought) to Bangalore from Mangalore. We quickly gobbled down our breakfast and got ready. I started feeling sick. But I realized that I could stop vomit by just taking a nap. Then whatever happens to me, my brain wouldn't know what I was feeling, so I won't vomit. And it actually worked! I think we had started around 9:00AM and ate some chips and other snacks, at 11:00AM I had fallen asleep in the car. And then I woke up at 2:00PM. I slept for three hours straight without any discomfort.

The reason why I had woken up was because of the honking of the cars in a traffic jam. My mother was desperately searching a place where we could eat lunch. My father had full eyes on the wheel so I thought to sleep a little more. But my father started talking to me a lot on purpose so I won't fall back to sleep. He said I should be active and was sleeping for a long time. I didn't say anything back. I was still groggy after the long nap.

My mother had finally found a restaurant where we could eat. But the restaurant's all seats were taken, but it was not very crowded. We decided to wait. My mind was wide awake now but my body wasn't. My body had turned into slime and if the serving guy wouldn't have minded, I would sat on the ground to wait.

Luckily, a seat was cleared and we sat. We ordered and the food came. The food was good. I asked my father about the distance from the restaurant to home. He said it was 45 mins. I would be finally rejoiced in the comfort of my home in 45 mins and sure enough, I did.

EIGHT

HISTORICAL SRIRANGAPATNA

We were going to a place where I have never even heard about. As usual, my parents didn't tell me where we were going so I had to find out myself. We started the trip at 11:00AM. As expected, it was very long which gave the usual nausea feeling. We were on the right path when my father mistakely missed a turn, but then, we saw a good restaurant. As it was lunch time, we ate there. It didn't take much time to reach the hotel from there. The hotel was different from what you think. The reception was outside the building where we stayed. Not outside the security gate. The room was good, with bad quality. It was a government hotel so my father said this was the best the government could do. My father went down to get some water bottles. My mother at that time opened the balcony. As soon as my mom stepped outside, monkeys came. There were like 15 monkeys waiting outside our balcony door. There were monkeys from the size of a 500ml bottle to the size of a table lamp.

I thought to show my father the scene when he comes back, but when I opened the balcony door, all the monkeys were gone, There was not even a single monkey nearby and now they were all gone like nothing ever happened. But when all the monkeys were gone, there was this beautiful view of the Kaveri River so near to our balcony, surrounded by natural forest, so that is one thing the government could give us.

Anyway, after all that we got freshen up. After resting a little while in the afternoon, we checked out a few places.

The first one was Tipu Sultan's summer palace. It had four entries (in which three of them were closed). It had a huge beautiful garden around it. I wondered, if his summer palace was this beautiful, how was his actual palace ? They showed all arts and all of which were boring. I just liked all the weapons and devices used in that time. They showed us some of Tipu's sofa and dining table. I don't think sofas and dining table can stay for 200 years and look new. So obviously they just remade it or polished it.

After that, we went to place number 2, Tipu Sultan's burial ground, which is called as Gumbaz. There were a lot of tombs around a temple like thing. The tombs were sizes of small to the size of an average adult.. Each was someone related to Tipu Sultan. In the temple like thing, there was Tipu's, his father's and his mother's tombs. Beside that there was a mosque. After coming out, I sat on a horse. which was uncomfartable. But then, the horse guy just left the horse on its own. It was scary, because it literally had a mind of its on. I mean, how would you feel when you and your family were going to the mall and suddenly, your car just speeds up for no reason. But luckily, I got down from the horse. It was dark, so we headed back to the hotel. We reached back at 7:00PM. We went down to dinner early because my father thought if we go early it'd be better. So we ate dinner and came back to our room. There were 3 cats roaming around. My father had some tea, made by me before he slept. I went to sleep at 10:00PM. The next day we had breakfast in a buffet. Which only had idli, sambar, vada. We had our buffet in a restaurant of the hotel, which was projected out on to the Kaveri river outside, so we were able to see the river flowing. After eating, we went for boating in the Kaveri river. The boat was round in shape. The sailor took a big round on the river. We could the see the houses on the other side. Small rocky islands were there in the river. After boating, we went to this temple of Vishnu sleeping. After that we went to a temple called Nimishamba temple. My legs started hurting. But then my mother got this magnificent idea of eating lunch in the temple with the ground burning in heat of the sun. After eating, my father ate some ripe jackfruit fruit no reason. Then we headed for destination three... or atleast we thought so. But it said its closing at 6:30PM, and it was 5:30PM, and it said it will take one hour to reach there. So we went to another place where Tipu's body was found. I thought it would be a big place but there was just one gravestone in the middle of a stone floor. In the gravestone it was written- "Tipu Sultan's body was found here". Nearby was a Kaveri river, the path to the river was through Tipu Sultan's old fort walls, so we went to see that. There were a lot of fishes in the water. It was evening so we went to a small restaurant to have some snacks. After eating some snacks, we went back to our room. After resting a little while, we went for dinner. After dinner we went back to room. I don't know if it is just me but I think when I saw the room first, it looked like garbage, but as the days went on, the room looked better. My father had some tea before he slept again. The next day, after eating breakfast, we were ready to leave. But before going back home, we had to see a temple. It was very clean because it was new. There were a lot of statues in. The ground was burning hot. This temple was built beside a dam on the Kaveri river. Then we ate lunch in a restaurant and went back home.

NINE

A Deep Trip (With the Same Friend)

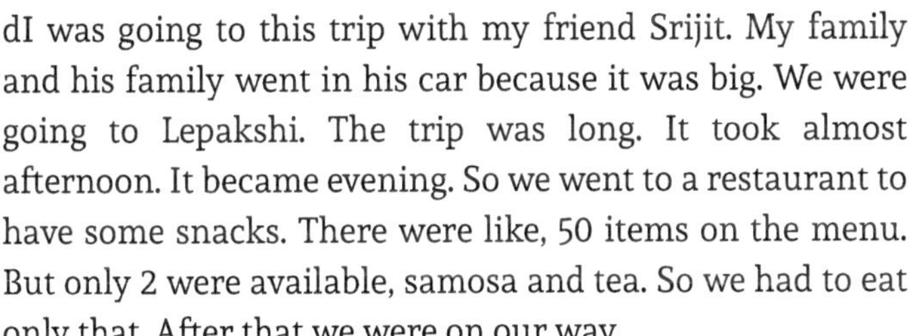

dI was going to this trip with my friend Srijit. My family and his family went in his car because it was big. We were going to Lepakshi. The trip was long. It took almost afternoon. It became evening. So we went to a restaurant to have some snacks. There were like, 50 items on the menu. But only 2 were available, samosa and tea. So we had to eat only that. After that we were on our way.

Suddenly, the cars started mysteriously disappearing behind and ahead of us. We had to drive for some time like this without any street light in the dark. Then GPS told us to take a road which was literally in the middle of a field. There was a small road which we found. So we went there. We were doubting if we were on the right path when suddenly, we found out resort. I wonder who the people there to take the garbage out, more importantly, how does the garbage truck come here? Anyways, it is already late, so we ate dinner there and went to sleep.

There was also indoor games in which me and Srijith played. The next day, we woke up a bit early. Because we were about to do some "sightseeing" aka just visit some places. Our place was a temple. So we ate our breakfast and went. There was this massive footprint in the temple which is supposed to be of hanuman. It was a very big temple.

But my father and Srijith's father was irritating us a lot of times to make us do meditation and all those things. Then we went to a Jatayu park. My mother and Srijith's mother went to see only the handicrafts there. It was very sunny. After that we went to a restaurant to eat lunch. After eating lunch, we went to eat some ice cream. But me and Srijith ate some hot chocolate brownie.

After that we went back to our resort. Then we played in the swimming pool a lot. Then we ate some snacks and went back to our rooms to freshen up. But then, Srijith's room toilet got clogged. So he had to shift to another room.

BUT he had another problem. The room which he got couldn't be locked. We were all very tired when we came back from the swimming pool. We were hungry, so we immediately ordered dinner. But they took a lot of time to get the dinner. Then the guys at the reception informed us that they have only one chef so he might take time. Then finally food arrived but myself and Srijith again went to play some more indoor games. We then had dinner and went to our respective rooms. The next day, we woke up late. Myself and Srijith saw a hidden park with some light gym equipments. They also had a bicycle which was broken. Then we again played some indoor games. This was our last day here. Finally we ate breakfast, took a bath and then we went back to Bangalore. On the way we ate lunch in a restaurant. Then we gave Srijith's car back. And then we came back to our house in our car.